HOLY WEEK & ME

HOLY WEEK & ME

Fr Bishoy Kamel

ST SHENOUDA PRESS
SYDNEY, AUSTRALIA
2024

Holy Week & Me
Fr Bishoy Kamel

COPYRIGHT © 2024
St. Shenouda Press

All rights reserved. Except for brief quotations in critical publications or reviews, no part of this book may be reproduced in any manner without prior written permission from the publisher.

ST SHENOUDA PRESS
8419 Putty Rd,
Putty, NSW, 2330
Sydney, Australia

www.stshenoudapress.com

ISBN 13: 978-1-7635450-0-7

All scripture quotations, unless otherwise indicated, are taken from the New King James Version®. Copyright © 1982 by Thomas Nelson, Inc. Used by permission. All rights reserved.

Contents

Introduction 7

Before Holy Week 15

Palm Sunday Eve 21

Palm Sunday 27

Monday & Tuesday 33

Wednesday 41

Thursday 47

Good Friday Eve 51

Good Friday 57

Introduction

It is without doubt that God's intention from His incarnation and life on earth, His entry in Jerusalem and His crucifixion was to free us from our enemy the devil; to rule in our hearts so that we enter His kingdom as His children and enjoy living with Him. This is the topic of our journey from His entry as a humble king riding a donkey to Jerusalem to His rise to govern on a wooden cross. "Say among the nations: the Lord reigns; the world also is firmly established; it shall not be moved; He shall judge the peoples righteously." (Psalm 96:10)

When the Lord made His triumphant entry into Jerusalem on Palm Sunday, the crowd joyously welcomed Him with palms, spreading their garments on the ground. The air echoed with shouts of "Hosanna to the King of Israel." As the Lord entered the town to establish His governance, it became evident that His kingdom was anything but ordinary: the adversary proved to be vicious. While the enemy's abilities were grounded in the material realm, Christ's transcended the spiritual. The battleground was the enemy's territory—the kingdom of this world. While the enemy's kingdom manifested visually, Christ's remained invisible. This, however, did not diminish its reality, for the visible is temporary, while the unseen is eternal. As we reflect on God's earthly journey, it unfolds before us, revealing His divine nature.

In every stage of His incarnation, Christ revealed His kingship:

First, In His Birth: Princes, the Wise Men, knelt before Him, offering their gold and seeking the born King of the Jews. Yet, our humble King Jesus, despite being pursued by Herod, chose an unexpected path, fleeing to Egypt. His homelessness, highlighted in Luke 1:7, carries an important message for the church. Christ, our King, is a stranger to the world, lacking a permanent home. A cautionary note for the church: clinging to worldly possessions jeopardises its connection with the estranged God. The humble and estranged God faced rejection from the Jews because He defied their expectations. Embracing Christ requires accepting Him as a different, rejected King. He reigns in the hearts of the humble, those willing to live an estranged life.

The prayer "Thy kingdom come..." echoes Christ's descent from heavenly glory to rule our hearts—a humble reign resembling the simplicity of the manger. This estrangement from a world He neither feared nor desired contrasts sharply with the rejected offers of the world. To invite Christ's reign, one must embody the humility of the manger—an unadorned sanctuary devoid of hierarchies, hatred, anger, or impurity. His world is full of purity, simplicity, and the innocence of lambs, mirrored in the unpretentious attire of Saint Mary and the shepherds. This stands in stark contrast to the complexities of the twentieth century.

Second, In His Entrance to Jerusalem: This pivotal scene unfolded with remarkable speed, surpassing the pace at which humans could follow. The Morning gospel reading on Palm Sunday emphasises the urgency: "Zachariah, hurry up and come down." This urgency signifies that the salvation incident transpired swiftly, and those who hesitated or failed to act promptly risked being overlooked. It marked the final opportunity for Jesus to pass through Zachariah's town, and only those who hurried could find Christ.

The events from Palm Sunday to the crucifixion unfolded with such gravity and solemnity that the world struggled to comprehend, in keeping with the prophecy in Zachariah 9:9 that highlighted the swift need for a donkey. We note several qualities of our King:

- **A Humble King:** Humility stands as the foremost and foundational attribute of King Jesus, who gracefully rides a donkey—a monarch for the humble and the children.

- **A King Who Reigns in Children's Hearts:** As Christ moved forward, joyous chants resonated from the hearts of children, much to the dismay of the Jewish leaders. Jesus, in his happiness, thanked the Father for revealing truths to the innocent while concealing them from the wise. We should implore Jesus to grant us the simplicity, honesty, and love of a child: without returning to childhood, we cannot enter God's kingdom. The complexities of our work and dealings with those who are not simple, coupled with the fears of our welfare and possessions, hinder our return. Yet, "out of the mouth of babes and nursing infants, You have ordained strength" (Psalm 8).

- **A King Who Cries:** Witnessing the city's ignorance of its salvation, Jesus wept. His tears fall not in vain; He cries at the doors of our hearts, revealing the ferocity of the unseen enemy and the peril that surrounds us, unknown to us. When we reject Christ, He stands before us, shedding tears for our hardness of heart and our ignorant minds, oblivious to our salvation. We must pray: my Lord Jesus, rise now, claim my heart with your tears, and let springs of tears burst forth.

- **A King with a Whip:** At the temple, Jesus barred entry

to those with unnecessary goods. Jesus guards the church doors, prohibiting entry of hearts burdened by worldly love, worries, and hatred. The priest must leave baggage outside, the deacon must forsake corruptible glory, and the youth must abandon love for the world and external beauty. Even the young are urged to leave certificates and studies outside, prioritising the search for the Kingdom and glory of God.

• A powerful king: As Jesus made his way into the city, a seismic energy reverberated. In Christianity, true strength manifests in the courage to self-regulate, fuelled by unwavering faith and profound love. Witnessing the crowd cast their garments beneath their feet symbolises the audacity to let go, a bravery exemplified by the saints. Today, the imperative is for Jesus Christ to reign over our hearts. The Holy Chrism has consecrated our bodies and souls, binding them to Christ. However, many of us, consecrated souls, still adorn ourselves with the garments of the world.

We must remember to ruthlessly strip off worldly attire, laying them at God's feet, acknowledging Him as the rightful King of our hearts. We must accept Him in His meekness, humility, rejection by leaders, and as a stranger to this world.

Third, King on The Cross: Sadly, many chanted and welcomed Christ as a King on Palm Sunday but the sincere ones who followed Him to the end were few, counted on the fingers of the hand. It is not sufficient to accept Christ as a meek King in our hearts, but we have to also carry the consequences of following His teachings. We have to carry His cross and follow Him at all times so that we rule with Him on the cross. He is the King to those who love Him.

Fourth, His Ascension: In the Lord's words, "You are from below, but I am from above" (John 8:23). The essence of ascension lies in the Lord's descent from above to save us from evil and draw us upward. The crucified Lord possesses a magnetic power far stronger than the world's desires and temptations, "...and I, if I am lifted up from the earth, will draw all peoples to Myself." The ascension journey is challenging, liberating us from worldly ties and propelling us forward, inviting others to join in the ascent to the highest realms of generosity, love, endurance, and humility. Christ willingly offered Himself to the priests who unknowingly crucified Him, becoming an offering for the entire world. "

As we follow Christ the servant, in his passion week, we are called to embrace suffering and pain. "The Son of Man has to suffer," declares the Gospel (Mark 8:31), which is done out of His genuine love for humanity. Just as a mother endures pain for her child, and a farmer toils in planting, Christ, out of love for us sinners, willingly bore the consequences of our sins—suffering and pain.

Let us recognise that suffering is not a punishment, but a gift bestowed upon those who love, serve, and ascend to the road of glory with Christ.

Before Holy Week

In Corinthians chapters 1 and 2, we read: "For Jews request a sign, and Greeks seek after wisdom, but we preach Christ crucified, to the Jews a stumbling block and to the Greeks foolishness. Yet, to both Jews and Greeks, Christ is the power and wisdom of God, surpassing the wisdom of men and the strength of God surpassing men's strength. In demonstration of the Spirit and power, we anchor your faith not in human wisdom but in the omnipotent power of God."

In a world where many are considered wise but few are strong or honorable, God intentionally chose the seemingly ignorant to shame the wise, the weak to shame the strong, and the lowly and despised to humble the esteemed. This strategic choice aims to dismantle human boasting in the presence of God.

When Jesus was on this earth, he deliberately avoided the use of complex words and human wisdom to proclaim His testimony. Similarly we should cast aside our fear, weakness, or dread because of a lack of human wisdom, but rely on the compelling proof of spiritual power. This approach ensures our faith is based on the enduring strength of God, to whom all glory belongs forever.

As we embark on the beautiful Holy Week, the Church's profound reverence for this time is evident through the extensive reading of scripture from the Old Testament. There exists a deliberate pattern in our church rituals, where readings from the New Testament are preceded by passages from the Old Testament. This intentional sequence highlights the intentional connection and, at times, the clarifying potency of the Old Testament over the New. Let us consider this poignant example: the events of Wednesday when a woman anointed Jesus with fragrant oil, while simultaneously, a conspiracy brewed among the Jews to betray Him. The intertwining of these narratives finds resonance in a psalm recited during this hour: "His words are softer than ointment but sharper than a sword." This psalm intricately weaves together the woman's anointing with fragrant oil and the sinister plot hatched by the Jews, revealing layers of meaning beyond the surface.

In our devotions, we immerse ourselves in the Psalms,

with particular emphasis on those of the Agpeya. These Psalms unfold various prophecies, not only concerning Christ's birth but also encapsulating the incidents of His life. A distinct prayer and praise for the power, glory, and honour of our Lord Jesus ("Thok te tigom...") replaces the traditional recitation of twelve psalms during this Holy week.

The Psalms, especially during moments like the crucifixion, unravel the mysteries and divine power encapsulated in Jesus Christ. The pivotal hour of His death on the cross, perceived as a moment of vulnerability, is poignantly depicted. A carefully chosen psalm for this moment, recited in half an hour, echoes the timeless truth: "Your throne, Lord, is forever and ever." This acknowledges that His reign is the cross, and the sceptre that guides this kingdom is imbued with significance. In essence, the recitation of this psalm delves into the depth of Christ's experiences, mirroring the intricacies expressed in the New Testament. The Old Testament, through its prophetic lens and poetic verses, serves as a portal, offering profound insights into the multifaceted narrative of Christ's journey, particularly during the climactic moments of His crucifixion.

The celestial symphony of Psalms assumes a pivotal role during the holy week, according to the profound insights shared by spiritual luminaries such as Saint Augustine. Their assertion, that the Psalms, from the first to the last, are a divine narrative of Christ, echoes through the sacred corridors of the Church. Consider the depth of in the first psalm, "Blessed is he who has not walked in the valley of the sinful." Only Christ remains untouched by the sinful valley. Our reliance on prophecies is evident, as every Old Testament reading is prefaced with foresight. Delving into Christ's crucifixion, we encounter a rich tapestry of prophecies, from the slaying of Isaac in Genesis to the moving imagery in the Psalms, describing hands and feet pierced, clothes divided, and a lamb led to slaughter.

Consider Christ's declaration to the thief on the cross—a profound moment that elicits varied interpretations. To some, Christ's apparent weakness might challenge the notion of salvation. Yet, we understand the divine unfolding. Christ's death on the cross becomes our gateway to paradise, an inheritance of eternal life. His resurrection, symbolises the transformative power of God's resurrection. In the final moments of His earthly journey, Christ, as a divine son, held all of humanity in His arms, entrusting it to the Heavenly Father. This pivotal act symbolised the church's perpetual embrace by the hands of the Heavenly Father—an exploration into the essence of this vital connection is our focal point.

Delving into matters of human wisdom, fraught with dangers and potential misdirection, the paradoxical image of Jesus on the cross emerges. Despite appearances of weakness, the thief on the right perceived a divine reality. In Christ's weakest moments, amidst scorn and plea for forgiveness, mysteries unfolded. The hymn "Amonoganees," chanted on Good Friday, reveals His strength in vulnerability.

Our salvation, encapsulated in God's power, calls for an exploration of this inherent strength. You and I seek the enduring power demonstrated by St Stephen – a strength seemingly feeble in the eyes of disciples. St Stephen, amidst persecution, gazed upon an opened sky, witnessing the Son of Man at the right hand of the Father. We look to St Paul to describe where such power comes from: the power is the cross. Although often rejected, the cross is the church's source of strength – it transcends outward symbols, beckoning a personal experience. St Paul's declaration, "I was crucified with Christ; it is no longer I who live, but Christ lives in me," encapsulates the essence of the cross as complete forgiveness from all our sins.

Christ's blood, symbolised by the cross, cleanses sins and imparts salvation. As we stand before the cross, let us don the white garment bestowed in baptism. The blood of Christ becomes a perpetual reminder, guiding souls to heaven – a communion of forgiven souls washed in the lamb's blood. Do not complain then about your evil sins, but instead courageously stand at the foot of the cross with thanksgiving and confess:

"Our Father, everything in me is bad, the blood of Christ is the only thing that can wash me and make me a new creation". None of us should think we cannot, or we are not worthy. Remember the right hand thief on the cross who was assured of his place in heaven because of his testimony.

The truth is that there is power in the cross. It is not human power: it is power of forgiveness; power of love; power of freedom in Christ. This was what apostle St Paul said: "I am crucified with Christ, I do not live but Christ lives in me."

Through the cross, you and I can remove the stress and anxiety from our heart. Worries about the future, your education or exams, your partner, or your physical appearance, your struggle with alcohol or substances. Or anything which occupies the heart. Saint Augustine said: "I have put my feet on the top of the world when I stopped fearing everything, not desiring anything and nothing frightens me." Nothing should frighten us too – not that we should become careless, but instead to become very full and content with Christ in my life. We should crucify the world with its desires and motives. Gaining the whole world means nothing compared to gaining Jesus. Remember St Paul was thrown into prison, but was singing hymns in the middle of the night. You and I can sacrifice anything but our freedom, therefore do not let anything worldly enslave you.

Palm Sunday Eve

The events of this week are full of good and important teachings. It was not clear when Christ said: "who wants to be my disciple, let him deny himself, carry his cross and follow me", but in the Passion Week Christ literally fulfilled what He said. If anyone wants to walk with Christ, let them follow these steps that Christ took, and they will not lose the way. The steps are very clear.

The incidents of this week are also very dangerous, because they happen with such speed. as important because they carry the speed essence. One incident was quickly followed by another. The last house Jesus entered before Ananias was the house of Zacchaeus the day before. He was passing by Aretha when He called Zacchaeus to hurry up and come down the tree. We saw how speed was of great importance in this incident. It was a life opportunity for Zacchaeus. If he were not to come down with hurry, Jesus was not going to pass by Aretha again. Occasions for salvation are speedy; if we do not catch them, they may pass away! Christ spent the day in Zacchaeus's house that day, then He travelled to the house of Anya, a town close to Jerusalem that Jesus liked to spend the night at. This was Christ's nature. He did not care about large cities as much as He did for small ones. The town was called Anya which means sick and poor. It had poor people surviving with hardship. Every day Christ was there, He taught new teachings. Interestingly, He did not ever spend a night in Jerusalem.

In the home of Ananias where Jesus shared supper prior to Passion week, Mary the sister of Lazarus expressed her appreciation by anointing Jesus's feet with costly ointment. Amidst daily tasks, she chose to sit at Jesus's feet, cherishing His words like precious treasures. Christianity, as Paul the Apostle eloquently articulated, is founded on love; he dedicated an entire chapter to extolling love's virtues, emphasising its primacy above all else. For Jesus, initiating the week with Mary's act of love underlined the centrality of love in worship. Without love, worship becomes mere obligation, devoid of meaning. Our sacraments, rooted in expressions of love for the Lord and His church, serve as tangible manifestations of this affection. Christ's love for humanity serves as the bedrock of our faith, inviting us

Palm Sunday Eve

into a relationship characterised by love and devotion.

While many followed Christ, few persevered to the end. Our journey behind Christ may lead us to trials, even death, but who will endure? Peter's denial of Christ serves as a poignant reminder that without love, our worship and deeds are hollow. Christ's probing question directed at him also applies to us too: "Do you love me?" Martyrs, driven by profound love for Christ, willingly sacrificed their lives. St. Augustine, disciple of Peter, yearned to prove his love through martyrdom, considering his blood a testament to his devotion. Throughout history, love for Christ has been the primary impetus for martyrdom and monasticism. Those consumed by this love found peace amid life's trials. Obstacles may arise, but what surpasses the cross or death? Only love can propel one beyond these barriers, to resurrection. Who, among the disciples, approached Christ after His crucifixion? Only one driven by love could brave the guards at the tomb. This devoted woman, restless on Saturday, hastened to Christ as soon as the Sabbath ended, earning the first revelation of His resurrection.

In essence, a path lacking love for Christ leads to stumbling. Amidst life's trials and worldly distractions, maintaining unwavering devotion is paramount. Believing one's heart is entwined with worldly matters is self-destructive. Apostle Paul prophesied that in the end times, people would become self-centred, prioritising love for themselves and money over devotion to God. In Christianity, love must be our cornerstone, epitomised by the cross upon which Christ sacrificed Himself. Through love, Christians establish a profound connection with Christ, essential for their spiritual journey. Walking the path of faith is difficult, especially amidst worldly temptations: maintaining purity, navigating modern challenges, or upholding Christian values in the face of societal pressures.

Yet, the Church endeavours to pave the way for Christ, the ultimate saviour by emphasising the importance of regular and contemplative reading of the Bible. Like David, who found delight and endless treasures in God's Word, Christians are encouraged to immerse themselves in its wisdom. For in the Word of God lies boundless joy, wisdom, and spiritual nourishment. When we truly love someone, we cherish their words, finding solace and guidance in them. Conversely, a lack of love for someone is reflected in indifference towards their words. Only those who have tasted the sweetness of God's Word and embraced it with sincerity are worthy companions on the journey with Christ. Mary's unwavering love for Jesus led her to choose the path of discipleship. St Paul, imprisoned for his faith, demonstrated the unbreakable bond of love between a believer and Christ. Despite his hardships, he remained steadfast in his love for Jesus, recognising that nothing could separate him from this love.

Palm Sunday Eve

The love of Christ is manifested in obedience to His teachings. As we internalize and obey His Word, Christianity becomes not just a religion, but a way of life filled with joy and purpose. Conversely, if we lack the energy and passion to love Christ, His commandments will seem burdensome and impractical. Christ's commandments are not heavy burdens for those who love Him. Rather, they are a source of strength and guidance, leading us to a life of fulfillment and spiritual richness. When we truly love Christ, His yoke becomes light, and His commandments become a joy to follow. Indeed, the road to glory is paved with challenges and crosses, but it is through the power of love that we navigate these obstacles and reach the ultimate destination. Just as Christ endured the cross and the grave before His resurrection, we too must embrace the trials of life with love and faith. We should pray for the love of God's Word to fill our hearts, knowing that it is the most precious possession that can never be taken from us.

Attendance at the mass is another crucial indicator of our love for Christ. Arriving late, feeling bored, or departing before the final blessing all show a lack of devotion. On the altar, Christ offers Himself as the ultimate act of love, inviting us to partake in His broken body and shed blood. How we respond to this invitation speaks volumes about our love for Him. When our minds wander during the mass, it's a reflection of our weakened love for Christ. If our hearts were truly consumed by love for the one who gave His life for us, distractions would fade away in the light of His love.

Actions during the mass, such as talking, distractions, or rushing through communion, reveal hearts devoid of understanding and love for the sacredness of the moment. A notable example is a devout worshipper I know, who after receiving communion, would retreat to his room for two hours, conversing with Christ whom he has eaten and was offered His blood. True worship, fuelled by love, transforms even the simplest acts into offerings of profound significance. Acts of service, when devoid of love, hold no value in the eyes of God. Whether it's offering financial contributions or forgiving others, the measure of their worth lies in the love behind them.

As we embark on Holy Week, let us open our hearts to the love of the cross and the journey of discipleship. May our worship be filled with the transformative power of Christ's love, elevating every aspect of our lives.

Palm Sunday

It is clear from all the readings in the four gospels that Christ had entered Jerusalem to reign over it and announce His kingdom. We cannot deny this point ever. Christ has come to establish a kingdom that is called the kingdom of Christ or the kingdom of Christians. If the Pharisees did not like this fact, He said to them: "I will let babes speak up and those who are suckling to announce it." They asked Him to silence his disciples. What was this story about a kingdom and a revolution and this upheaval you are claiming you will do? He told them that even if his disciples were silenced, the stones will talk.

The scene of Christ coming down the mount of Jerusalem with the people following Him looked like a king entry conquering a city. People were not only behind Him but in front and behind; much like a chorus of deacons chanting before and after Him. The first chorus enchanting: "Blessed is the king of Israel" and the second: "Hosanna in the highest." Christ emerged on earth to establish His reign. Recall the account of His birth: the Wise Men saw a star in the East, signalling the arrival of the king of the Jews. Journeying to Jerusalem, they sought the newborn which led them to a humble manger, where they found not a regal spectacle, but a modest child. This juxtaposition echoes the scene of Palm Sunday—a lowly donkey bearing a remarkable figure, revered by the masses.

Although born in simplicity, Christ received worship fit for royalty. Kings humbled themselves before Him, offering gifts of gold, frankincense, and myrrh in recognition of His divine kingship. Notably absent were the trappings of earthly sovereignty—a blatant departure from conventional royals. Christ's kingship defied earthly norms; He wielded an olive branch rather than a sword, demanded no tribute, and yet His reign was inevitable as evidenced by Herod's extreme reaction. Perhaps Herod sensed the child's future kingship, agitated further by whispers from the devil. Desperate to thwart this perceived threat, Herod committed the heinous act of slaughtering Bethlehem's innocent newborns. When Christ was tempted on the mount by the devil, He absolutely rejected offers of worldly power. Unlike earthly rulers hungry for dominion, Christ chose a reign characterised by love, humility, service, and righteousness. It is fair to say that that the glory of His kingdom is veiled to the worldly-minded but revealed to those who embrace His divine purpose

Jesus Christ's rising popularity and expanding discipleship caused much worry among the Pharisees and scribes. Initially, His followers comprised humble fishermen and marginalised women, including Mary Magdalene whom Christ liberated from seven demons, and tax collectors deemed societal outcasts. Nevertheless, their ranks swelled over time, particularly after the miraculous resurrection of Lazarus, a feat unparalleled in their midst. Christ's reign, as prophesied by David, transcends earthly dominion to encompass the realm of hearts. Unlike conventional kingship, focused on worldly power, Christ's kingdom operates on a different plane. Even when Pilate interrogated Him about his aspirations for kingship, Christ affirmed His noble status, He said: "my kingdom is not from this world."

The trajectory of Christ's reign, from His humble birth heralded by shepherds to His proclamation as King of the Jews, highlights His divine mission. Zechariah's prophecy of a king entering Jerusalem on a young colt further describes the humble nature of Christ's kingship. In Jewish prayers, the anticipation of God's kingdom was paramount, with the invocation "your kingdom come" serving as a cornerstone. Apostle

Matthew, addressing a Jewish audience, emphasised this, referencing "the kingdom of God" or "the kingdom of heaven" extensively throughout his gospel. St Matthew's deliberate choice to trace Christ's lineage to David underscores the enduring significance of Davidic kingship, a motif echoed in contemporary references to the "Star of David" and "kingdom of David."

Acknowledging Christ as king is intrinsic to our faith. The proclamation "Blessed is He who comes in the name of God" resounds whenever scripture is read aloud in church, reminiscent of the accolades bestowed upon Christ during His triumphal entry. Importantly, Christ's reign extends beyond earthly realms; His triumph over the devil (through His crucifixion) inaugurated His kingdom. The devil's claim over humanity, rooted in Adam's transgression, was nullified by Christ's sacrificial offering. St Paul's epistle to the Colossians explains this victory, describing Christ's act of redemption as the annulment of a "legal letter of debt," liberating humanity from bondage. The Holy Communion, symbolising the "banquet of the thousand years," typifies our participation in Christ's kingdom, transcending temporal boundaries. Furthermore, the fearless demeanour of the martyrs, faced with threats of violence, demonstrated a strength which transcends human capacity and defies earthly powers.

As heirs to Christ's kingdom, believers are reminded of

their worth, bought with the blood of Christ. Despite worldly disdain or loss, our value remains rooted in our membership within Christ's body, the church. The essence of Christ's kingdom lies in love: the hallmark of His disciples and the rock of the church. Without love, the kingdom falters, for as Christ taught, "By this everyone will know that you are my disciples, if you love one another." Thus, love becomes the adhesive binding believers to Christ and to one another, sustaining the unity of the body. Our membership in Christ's kingdom is a sacred privilege, bestowed through His sacrificial love. As heirs of this kingdom, let us cultivate pure and unwavering love in our hearts. As brothers and sisters, bound by the blood of Christ, we must uphold this sacred bond with integrity.

Just as Judas succumbed to the lure of material wealth, so too are we warned against the seductive appeal of worldly pursuits. Betrayal, whether through moral compromise or defiance of Christ's teachings, is against our allegiance to Christ and His church. In a world tainted by sin and moral decay, devotion to Christ's kingdom becomes vital. St Paul's appeal to avoid conformity to worldly standards echoes this sentiment. To emulate the values and pursuits of the earthly world is to court spiritual peril, for one cannot serve both God and worldly desires. We must remember that our lives are not our own, but rather a holy offering to the One who purchased us with His blood. Our children, our possessions, our very beings – all belong to God, entrusted to us as stewards of His kingdom.

Though we may be but a small flock, we are owned by the King of kings, heirs to His eternal kingdom. As temples of the Holy Spirit, we find fulfillment in Christ alone; our hearts ignited with love for our Saviour. Let our lives be a testament to this devotion; just as they did on Palm Sunday, let our mind and souls be filled with praise for the King who reigns over us. Let us pray fervently that hypocrisy finds no roots within us, so that our commitment to Christ remains steadfast and true.

Monday & Tuesday

One of the most famous incidents at the start of Holy Week is the cursing of the fig tree, which despite its appearance did not bear any fruit. Christ our saviour is warning us about hypocrisy. As Jesus confronted the barren fig tree, it represents our spiritual emptiness cloaked in outward piety. Just as the fig tree withered under His curse, so too will those who neglect the cultivation of inner virtue. Similarly, in response to the Pharisee's astonishment when Christ and His disciples neglected the customary handwashing before meals, He replied by teaching that outward purity paled in comparison to inner integrity. He likened those who prioritise external appearances to whitewashed tombs – beautiful on the outside but concealing decay within.

Throughout the readings the theme of the fig tree

recurs. Isaiah's prophecy depicted God's tender care for His vineyard, yet despite His diligent cultivation, it yielded only bitter fruit. The question becomes what more could God have done? Indeed, when effort fails to yield expected results, disappointment follows. Worldly distractions and fretting over temporal concerns stifle our spiritual vitality.

In the readings from Genesis, we revisit humanity's first disobedience: the fall of Adam and Eve. Seduced by the promise of godlike knowledge, they succumbed to sin, seeking to cover their shame with fig leaves. Thus, the once again the fig tree symbolises human folly, the inadequacy of self-made righteousness.

At this stage of Holy week, we contemplate the fate of Jerusalem which is symbolic of spiritual barrenness; we are reminded of our own spiritual pilgrimage. Planted in the heavenly paradise of the Church, we are called to bear fruit worthy of our calling. Here the connection to the fate of the fig tree emphasises that external appearances are fleeting and true righteousness emanates from within. We must learn from the mistake of the fig tree: cultivating spiritual fruitfulness will allow us to stand firm, rooted in the grace of God, bearing fruit that endures for eternity.

Saint Shenouda, the leader of hermits, questions the disparity between the paradise God envisioned and the outside world: how can the Church differ so much from the earthly realm. Reflecting on Adam's sin and its repercussions, he highlighted the need for purification from the curse that befell creation due to human transgression. Through Christ's sacrifice, this curse was lifted, blessing all creation with His redeeming blood. Drawing a parallel between Adam's expulsion from paradise and the fate of the barren fig tree, Saint Shenouda stressed the importance of bearing spiritual fruit. Rebuking the Pharisees' preoccupation with outward appearances, Jesus repeatedly urged them to focus on justice, mercy, and faith—qualities that define true righteousness.

St Paul teaches us about our sacredness as a vessel of honour. By grace we are the temple of God and His spirit lives in us; the one who corrupts the temple of God, God will destroy because the temple is holy. Those who defile their bodies or harbor resentment toward others, he warned, ultimately desecrate the temple of God within them. Saint Shenouda reminds us that just as Christ condemned the corruption within the temple, so too must individuals safeguard the sanctity of their bodies, which houses the Holy Spirit. Just as Adam and Eve attempted to hide their shame with fig leaves, so too must individuals confront their inner failings before God. In the eyes of God, true beauty lies not in outward appearances but in the purity of the heart.

God revealed to the prophet Ezekiel the hidden transgressions of the priests through a hole in the temple – the unclean things they were doing inside and how priests dared offering incense with their backs to the altar. Once again outward piety is contrasted with inward corruption. Despite outward displays of worship, their hearts remained distant from God's true teachings. Our lives are sacred, cherished vessels for the Holy Spirit bestowed upon us by our Lord Jesus Christ. We must honour and respect our bodies as temples, ensuring that even the food we consume nurtures our internal sanctity. God will hold accountable those who defile His temple, as He dwells within each of us.

Our Lord Jesus Christ gave each of us a Holy Body, a temple that He came and lives inside. How do we honour and respect it? We should go so far as to say that even the food that we eat should be holy. If anything harms our body, it is also harmful to our spiritual life. Contrary to the world's obsession with external appearances, the Church emphasises the cultivation of internal virtues. Although societal pressures may compel us to conform to external standards, Christ calls us to transcend these worldly norms and embody His divine principles. Consider weddings, a blessed sacrament before God's altar. After one wedding, the party that followed involved revelry and debauchery afterward which betrays the sanctity of the sacrament. Such actions reflect a prioritisation of outward appearances over internal righteousness, a trend prevalent in today's society.

As Christians, we possess one life – one that must reflect our allegiance to Christ. Our existence is intertwined with His, and our actions should mirror His teachings. When Christ demands spiritual fruit from us, we must heed His call, lest we face the consequences of spiritual barrenness. The path to holiness is within reach, requiring faith, dedication, and love for our Lord. Christ desires single-hearted devotion, rejecting the divided allegiance of a heart torn between Him and the world.

Our teacher Paul said in his letter to Colossian " We have risen with Christ, seek those things that are from above... not on things on the earth." Creating a holy environment within our homes does not necessitate a life of deprivation but rather a prioritisation of spiritual values over worldly pursuits. Instead of the television that is always on with obscene films, use it for religious viewing. Instead of being worried about your children's success or education, care first about their spiritual life and what will benefit them in heaven. By replacing worldly distractions with Godly influences, we nurture an atmosphere conducive to spiritual growth.

In our church, and among its servants, there must be vigilant care. Those standing at the altar should fix their gaze upon Christ, unwavering in devotion. If we engage in church rituals with wholehearted sincerity, our lives will abound with blessings. Yet, often, during the reading of Gospel, we are physically present but spiritually absent, disregarding the deacon's call to "Stand up in the fear of God and listen to the Holy Gospel".

The altar, known as "the Door of the King" is a sacred space reserved solely for the priest. Its sanctity demands reverence, for it is God's dwelling place. The Eucharist, symbolised by a burning ember from the altar, purifies and absolves sin upon contact with the lips. Yet, some members of the congregation depart during Communion, which means they do not truly feel Jesus is present. Moreover, we must remember that God desires spiritual fruitfulness in our lives.

Ask yourself this: do you think God gave you life in this world to live to become a doctor, or an engineer, or a teacher, or any other profession in the society? Would you be content to leave this world with your current level of cultivated spiritual fruit? While earthly pursuits like professional success may hold value to help the sick or teach young children, true fulfillment lies in bearing spiritual fruit; Christ says "I want spiritual fruit." Apostle St Paul said: "the fruit of the Holy Spirit is love, joy, peace, longsuffering, gentleness, goodness and faith." We are admonished to strive for spiritual excellence, warning against the allure of worldly distractions. Christ urges us to prioritise spiritual growth and readiness for His return, lest we be found wanting on the Day of

Judgment.

In the sixth hour readings, we were told to strive to enter from the narrow road before it is closed. There will be people who come once it is too late and try to enter, saying they have expelled devils in Christ's name and perhaps even greater things, but He will say to them that He does not know them. Let us heed this warning to earnestly seek spiritual renewal, yielding a bountiful harvest of righteousness. Beware of entering eternity without any spiritual fruit, for such a fate would be regrettable indeed. Let us, therefore, diligently cultivate spiritual richness within ourselves, knowing that our fruitfulness blesses not only us but also those around us. Our worship should not merely appease onlookers but should be genuine towards our Heavenly Father, who sees the depths of our hearts.

As the Lord evaluates our lives, may He find them fruitful, rooted by the streams of living water and bearing fruit in due season. Just as He hungered for figs while on earth, so too does He desire spiritual fruit from the lives He has planted. In the Song of Songs, it says that He ate from the fruit; the cherished one from the inside. After eating, He said to His friends, come let us eat and drink from the cherished fruit. How precious is the fruitful church that has the aroma of Christ which stands in stark contrast to the barrenness of the world, pleasing the heart of the Lord.

Wednesday

The last day Jesus spends with the crowd is Tuesday, and from Wednesday onwards he spends His time with his disciples. Today the Lord spoke about the second coming and how that day will be fearful for those souls who rejected Him, but at the same time it will be a joyful day for the souls waiting for Him.

Among the most poignant narratives in the Gospel is the account of a woman anointing Jesus with fragrant ointment, a tale recounted in Matthew, Mark and Luke. Mary, Lazarus's sister, poured ointment on Jesus's feet before the Passover by six days; but today a different lady poured ointment on the Lord's head.

As the woman anointed Jesus, a simultaneous act of betrayal was unfolding. Judas conspired to betray the

Lord for thirty pieces of silver. Jesus acknowledges the woman's act of devotion, recognizing it as a precursor to His impending burial. The woman's gesture parallels Christ's own sacrificial offering, as both pour themselves out: she, with precious ointment, and He, with His very life. Though the disciples remained oblivious to the impending events, the woman's love transcended human understanding. Her actions, driven by profound love, foreshadowed Christ's sacrificial death.

Christ's love, exemplified by His selfless sacrifice, extends beyond human comprehension. Despite the bitterness of betrayal, it is ultimately inconsequential in the face of such boundless love. Christ applauds her by saying wherever the Bible is preached in the world, this woman will be remembered for what she has done.

In contemplating the nature of Christ's love, we are drawn to the imagery found in Chapter 1 of Song of Solomon: "Let Him kiss me with the kisses of his mouth for thy love is better than wine. Because of the aromatic of thy good ointments, thy name is an ointment poured forth." Christ's love knows no bounds, embracing even the most sinful and unworthy. Unlike human love, which may waver in the face of wrongdoing, Christ's love remains steadfast and unwavering. If our love for Him surpasses all earthly affections, we have truly grasped the essence of Christianity.

Christ has never rejected any of us, nor treated any of us badly even though we have all betray Him many times. Is there any one more tender than Christ? Can anyone love us more than Christ? David said: "if my father and mother left me, the Lord accepts me." Christ loves us even when we are bad and sinful. He loves us when we hurt Him and even if we curse Him. He said: "When you pray, go into your room, and when you have shut your door pray for Your Father who sees in the secret place and Your Father who sees in secret will reward you openly."

Let us centre our worship with God on this profound truth: to reciprocate Christ's love, recognising that He loved us unconditionally and gave Himself for our sake. Our worth in Christ's eyes, as sinful beings, equals the preciousness of His blood. His arms remain open to welcome us back, regardless of our past transgressions, demonstrating His infinite grace and forgiveness. May our daily prayers and devotions be more than mere recitations but rather offerings of love, similar to the ointment poured out.

Our love for Christ should manifest in our eagerness to immerse ourselves in His word. Let our desire to read Scripture match our love for Him, reflecting a personal commitment to deepen our relationship with Christ. Do we love Christ as He loves us, unconditionally and sacrificially? Will we endure hardships for His sake, exhibiting acts of love in secret, fostering an intimate bond with Him?

In essence, Christianity without the fragrance of love is incomplete. Let us move beyond superficial displays of devotion and embrace the transformative power of love, poured into our hearts by the Holy Spirit. Love is not merely a sentiment but an action that can be consumed, much like the bread broken by Christ Himself. Through the Holy Communion, we partake in His love. What greater gift could He offer than Himself? Judas's descent into treachery was not sudden but gradual, stemming from his misguided priorities. Unlike forgiven sinners such as Peter, whose love for Christ endured despite their failings, Judas's heart was devoid of love, consumed instead by the appeal of position and recognition.

Christ's entry into Jerusalem, humble yet resolute, underlines the purity of His mission: to claim the hearts of His people, rather than earthly glory. Similarly, our devotion should be untainted by ulterior motives, rooted solely in love for our Saviour. The disciples, too, grappled with this concept, when we hear about their squabbles over positions of honour. Peter and Judas's rivalry for seats of prominence at the Last Supper serves as a cautionary tale against the pitfalls of seeking status in the Kingdom of God.

In the depths of weakness, St Paul found strength through the grace of Christ, discovering that true power emerges when we surrender our vulnerabilities to the Almighty. His conclusion after enduring hardships and tribulations was: "When I am weak, then I am strong," which summarises the paradoxical nature of faith. Contrastingly, Judas's heart, devoid of genuine love for Christ, exemplifies the danger of betrayal of the heart itself. His act of selling Christ for a paltry sum echoes a profound disregard for the Saviour's worth, reducing Him to the value of a slave in his eyes. For you and I, we must refrain from the subtle betrayals that creep into our daily lives: the distractions that divert our attention from the sacred. In a world consumed by materialism and worldly pursuits, it is love, not intellectual understanding, that truly reveals the essence of Christ.

Consider, too, the worth we assign to Christ in our daily routines. When the busyness of life consumes our time and attention, when His Word remains unopened and His presence unacknowledged, are we not, in essence, diminishing His value in our lives? Let us heed the cautionary tale of Judas and strive to elevate Christ's worth in our hearts, especially as we age and face the temptations of complacency. Whether in the vigour of youth or the wisdom of age, let our devotion to Christ deepen.

Do not be deceived by a false sense of security in

religious duties, for even Judas, among Christ's closest disciples, fell victim to such pride. Let us, instead, commit ourselves to seeking the fragrant ointment of His love in every aspect of our lives. On reflection of the events of today, let us build a relationship with Christ which is characterised by clarity and sincerity. Let us not be swayed by the temptations of worldly praises but remain steadfast in our devotion, confident that God's glory can shine even through our weaknesses.

Thursday

How splendid is this day! A day adorned with the wondrous deeds of the Lord, surpassing all earthly measure. Are we, mere mortals, truly deserving of the Lord's profound acts of grace? Can we fathom the depth of humility in His washing of our feet, the boundless love symbolised in His offering of His body and blood? None among us can claim worthiness for such divine benevolence. Even the Cherubim, veiling their faces in reverence, cannot behold His glory. How incomprehensible that He, transcending the celestial realms, would descend to a stable for our sake!

Passover Thursday, the pinnacle of the Church's glory, bears heavenly significance. The events of today foreshadow the imminent sacrifice tomorrow. Though some may perceive Christ as captive, the truth reveals

His voluntary surrender. Today, our Lord offers Himself willingly, symbolizing not only the Eucharist but also His forthcoming sacrifice on the cross: a Passover for all humanity.

Recall the jubilant cries of "Hosanna" that echoed through the streets on Palm Sunday. Christ must reign supreme in our hearts and minds to establish His holy kingdom within us. As the Bible says, He shall make us kings and priests, ruling through the force of His boundless love. Traditionally, kings assert power through the might of swords and spears, yet Christ's reign is unlike any other. His conquest is not of land or riches, but of hearts and souls, as we read in the Song of Solomon: "Turn your eyes away from me, for they have overcome me." Such is the power of His love, it conquers without force.

Even as Christ, the exalted King, entered Jerusalem on a humble donkey, the Jews failed to recognise His humility, mocking instead of revering Him. His faithful children however know Him as the glorious King of Kings, fulfilling the prophecy of Zechariah: "Do not be afraid daughter of Zion. Here is your king coming humble and triumphant, riding on a colt." This grand design, orchestrated by God's divine wisdom, aims to redeem humanity from the devil's ownership. Through simple yet profound acts, the Holy Spirit draws us from the clutches of darkness into the radiant light of Christ's love. Consider the courage of Moses, who pleaded with the Lord on behalf of His people, despite their faithlessness. Are they worthy of the Rock that sustained them, of Christ's side that flowed with living water? In the face of such ingratitude, Moses dared to intercede, offering himself in exchange for their redemption.

Compare the Prophet Moses and Christ: Moses, in his plea to God, offered to forfeit his place in the Book of Life for the salvation of his people. However, God revealed that the true Saviour, the incarnate Word, would not succumb to death but would grant life. The actions of Moses resemble the sacrificial nature of Christ's mission. As Isaiah poetically expressed, He who encompasses the world and its inhabitants chose a lowly birthplace, finding no lodging but a stable.

Consider, if someone were to kneel and kiss your feet, you might flinch at such humility. Yet, Christ, the Lord of Lords, humbled Himself to wash the feet of His disciples, including Judas, who would betray Him. This act of humility defies human logic! Jesus, who fed Judas, bent to wash his feet – a gesture of unfathomable grace. If we take a minute to reflect on this action, we realise we are unworthy of such humility. Yet, Christ, in His boundless love, tells us He will continue to bend and wash our feet, despite our countless betrayals and sins. How can we not yield our hearts completely to Him? Despite our transgressions, He never turns away. How can we not become Your devoted servants? Is there any power or allure in this world that should vie for kingship in our hearts? I resoundingly declare: NO. Nothing should rival Christ's reign in our hearts.

Christ is our Saviour and King. He offers Himself to us – breaking His body and shedding His blood. Our meditation should be on the significance of this sacrifice. We may be blessed with strength, health, or prosperity, but more than that we are given Christ himself freely. Though none among us may match Judas's betrayal, there are those who approach Your table with impure hearts and still, Christ's love remains undiminished. As Saint Gregory writes, "There is no power of utterance that can limit Your love to the Human beings "

In the face of His love, what can we offer? Every time we approach, burdened with sin and betrayal, He graciously offers Himself. So what can we do in return? Even the woman who anointed You fell short. As St Ignatius professed, " I will never sense that I love Christ if I did not shed my blood same like He did for me." Let us revere the One who washed our feet, loved us, and sacrificed Himself. Respect and awe are due to Him and His house. May we honour His Body, Blood, and the humility He displayed to fully appreciate the gratitude of His sacrificial love.

Good Friday Eve

The events of this momentous day, truly surpass the sum of all the world's books. With the grace of the Holy Spirit, we should not dwell on the number of incidents of this day, but instead fix our gaze upon Jesus Christ and His profound offering. Each of us will receive a different lesson directly from the Lord's heart, attempting to grasp the intricacies of the Saviour's emotions. The Bible depicts Him a human just like you and I: amazed, sorrowful, distressed, and praying fervently till sweat was falling like blood drops on the ground. It is of course very difficult for us to fully comprehend His feelings. When St Peter cursed Him, Christ, with a compassionate glance, saved him. Who among us can put themselves in Christ's shoes and tolerate the intense emotions when the traitor Judas, with a deceitful kiss, delivered Him to the chief priests and scribes? Or when He endured slaps, spitting, and mockery, yet spoke not a word in anger?

Christ summarised these trials succinctly to those arresting Him at night, "This is your hour and the power of darkness." As we focus on the events that happened, let us reflect on Christ's preceding humility to wash the feet of His disciples, knowing the impurities of their hearts and upcoming denial and betrayal. He, to whom is due all glory such that the Cherubim must cover their face, stooped to cleanse our sins and renew the essence of life through His broken body and shed blood.

Tonight's events, recorded in each of the four Gospels, are pivotal. After supper and hymns, Christ retreated to the Mount of Olives. In the Gospel of John, chapters fourteen through seventeen, we find a treasure trove of Christ's teachings and prayers for every generation. Though completely sinless, Jesus prayed fervently, and His prayer from this night is added to the prayers used by the church. As He took Peter, James, and John to Gethsemane, His distress grew evident. His prayers, initially calm, intensified as He faced the impending cup – the hour of darkness. Although nothing had happened yet, the Lord knew what was going to happen. The cup symbolises the lethal poison of humanity's sins. In the Old Testament, when Israel disobeyed, God sent serpents whose poisonous bite caused death. Christ foresaw this cup – the poison of sin – and the excruciating ordeal ahead.

In the presence of God, Jesus beheld the sins of all generations, past and present, mirrored in the cup before Him. He confronted the looming hour of darkness. What did Christ do? He stood to pray, His supplications akin to blood-stained sweat, and said His famous words: "if you wish Lord to pass this cup from Me, not according to my will but Yours." Christ, in His divine glory, unveiled the unbearable weight of this cup, a precursor to the cross itself. He did not ask for it to be removed, but wanted to reveal to us that this cup is truly unbearable by any other human.

Today, His sweat fell as blood drops, willingly shedding His blood to cleanse the poison of our sins. This offering signifies His unwavering presence in our darkest hour. He invited His disciples to pray with Him, urging attentiveness rather than sleep to be prepared for the impending trials. Often, we misconstrue prayer as a gift to Christ. However, it is a means for us to endure the hour of darkness orchestrated by Satan, sustained by His intercession. We all face countless trials and worldly temptations; familial strife, spiritual apathy, and youth struggles – all are moments of darkness. Yet, Peter's sword in the garden, symbolic of human efforts shows, us that true armour against evil lies not in physical weaponry but in spiritual strength. Against such forces, prayers stand as our only weapon. Christ assures us that he will be beside us when facing our struggles.

Now, let us ponder: Did Christ's prayer remove that cup? Did it conquer the darkness's hold over humanity? No, it did not; so what transpired? While Christ Himself required no strengthening, the support of the angel demonstrated that our prayers, tears, and supplications do not fall on deaf ears. Angels come to strengthen us in our trials. When angels strengthen us, what follows? The hour of darkness remains, yet we traverse it in peace. Peter fell into the trap of cursing and was embarrassed as he heard the rooster's crow, and after weeping bitterly he emerged unscathed by genuine repentance. Importantly, our prayers do not abolish the hour of darkness, but rather recruit additional heavenly strength to endure them. The Church, adorned with Christ's power and glory, prevails against darkness as described in the Song of Solomon: "Who is this coming up from the wilderness, Leaning upon her beloved?" This is our church, pure like the sun and beautiful like the moon.

Consider the example set by St George. Despite his young age (only 20 years old) he remained steadfast in faith and purity in the face of temptation by a prostitute. He was sustained by the Spirit of the Lord, and this young lady who was sent to tempt him into sin repented from her ways and followed the Lord also. We too have Christ by our side to emerge victorious from darkness, radiant and unblemished. We will come out perfumed with myrrh and incense.

Good Friday Eve

As Christ concluded His earthly struggle, He prays one last 'farewell' prayer. The one sitting at the head of the Cherubim, who rode the colt, who was born in a manger, who fasted for us forty days and forty nights, who was tempted by the devil, who washed Judas's feet in the morning, who broke His body and gave us His love and offered us eternal life; what did He say in His farewell prayer? As we read in the Gospel of John: "I am not asking only for those but also for all who will believe in me so that they all become one as You are in me, My Father and I am in You, so that they also become one in us." He implored the Father to unify believers as He was unified with God. This unity, the culmination of Christ's sacrifice, was His ultimate desire: that humanity would be one with God. Did you anticipate that Christ's earthly struggle, His prayers, supplications, and all His deeds would culminate in our unity with God? No one could imagine the position we would attain after this struggle and what Jesus offered.

Through the events of tonight, Christ unveiled His new covenant that we become members of the body of Christ. He likened Himself to a vine and us to branches, underlining the necessity of remaining connected to grow and bear fruit. This invitation extends a completely undeserved heavenly grace and a share in Christ's glory. As our teacher apostle St Paul said when Christ shows in our lives, we will show in glory with Him. In this way we understand our worth: He desires the same love that the

Father had for Him to reside within us.

Did you imagine that the flawed, vulnerable human could unite with Christ? St Paul urged us to be clothed in Christ, and Christ Himself declared that consuming His body and blood unites us with Him. This was Christ's plea to the Father – to unify us and grant us the same glory He received. Christ prayed for our preservation and asked His Father to glorify us in His truth, as He glorified Himself for us.

With this in mind, we can grasp the essence of Scripture: unity with the Father, membership in Christ's body, and passage through our periods of darkness into His glory. Let us glorify Him for His abundant mercy, singing praises to the Lord who became our great and blessed Saviour.

Good Friday

Today is a solemn yet significant festival day. Though the church appears sombre and mournful, with sad hymns and mouths parched from fasting, these preparations lead to the bitter herbs to be consumed at Passover. Yesterday, we reflected on the profound humility of Our Lord, Jesus Christ, as He humbly washed the feet of all – including Judas – despite humanity's sinful nature. He bestowed upon us His divine love, offering Himself as the ultimate expression of love and anchoring us in Him, granting us eternal life.

As St John recorded, Christ was brought before Pilate at the sixth hour which corresponds to noon, the same time preparations for the Passover were underway. In his letter to the Corinthians, Apostle Paul explains that Passover is a feast for the Jews, but Christ is our Passover since it was the day Christ was slaughtered for us. In fact, "Pascha" is the Coptic word meaning Passover.

Although we refer to the whole week as the Pascha, the original Passover is described in Exodus 12: The Lord told Moses and Aaron in the land of Egypt saying: 'This month becomes the beginning of all months. It shall be the first month of all the year for you.' All the Israeli groups keep a lamb with them from the tenth day to till the fourteenth of the same month. Then on the evening of that last day that they start slaughtering the lamb, take the blood and put it on the two side posts and upper door post of their houses where they eat it. They eat the flesh that night, roast with fire with unleavened bread and bitter herbs. The reason for the bitterness is to remind them of the unfavourable and unappreciative traits of mankind, especially when God gives us blessings without any hardship. Similarly, our solemnity today represents the bitter herbs of Christ (our Passover) to appreciate the blessings God is bestowing upon us.

God instructed the Israelites to eat the Passover meal with urgency, their belts girded, shoes on their feet, and staffs in hand, signifying readiness for departure. Pharaoh and his people awoke to great mourning and cries of anguish as every first born in Egypt was struck by God, sparing only those protected by sacrificial blood on their door posts. The Lord's instructions were specific that the Passover was only for God's people who were first circumcised, equivalent to Christianity's baptism. They then left the land of Egypt, carrying the memory of the blood on their doorposts. Although a direct route via the Gulf of Suez would have been quicker, God in His wisdom led them into the wilderness were they had to cross the Red sea to enter Sinai. By Moses's command, the sea was miraculously parted, allowing them to pass safely while Pharaoh and his soldiers were destroyed.

Understanding the significance of the blood from the original Passover, you and I are spared from the power of the angel of death by Christ's blood on the cross. "As for you also, Because of the blood of your covenant, I will set your prisoners free from the waterless pit" (Zachariah 9:11). Through Christ's blood, millions of believers who died before Christ (waiting in hell) were freed from captivity. St Peter through the Holy Spirit clarifies this for us "For Christ also suffered once for sins, the just for the unjust, that He might bring us to God" (1 Peter 3:18).

For this reason, today is not one of only sorrow but also of jubilation. St Paul reminds the Colossians in chapter 2 of Christ's triumph over sin "In Him you were also circumcised with the circumcision made without hands, by putting off the body of the sins of the flesh, by the circumcision of Christ, buried with Him in baptism, in which you also were raised with Him through faith in the working of God, who raised Him from the dead."

Christ came with His blood and announced the good news to the souls in captivity, the souls that were in hell, and erased the debt that burdened us since Adam. Christ's payment of this debt was beyond the capacity of prophets, saints, or religious leaders. Satan himself would have said that it was a very expensive debt on all the lives of every human being to ever walk on the earth.

Liberation of humanity from Satan's grip is central to Christian theology. God, in His fairness and justice, orchestrated a divine plan to redeem mankind from the bondage of sin. This plan culminated in the sacrificial death of Jesus Christ on the cross. Through His selfless act of laying down His life, Christ aimed to abolish the liability deed of sin that burdened all of humanity and offered the promise of salvation. The cross for the Christians is not a disgrace, but a strength.

The death of Christ on the cross did not change the nature of Satan, the death of Christ on the cross provided protection for man against Satan. St James tells us that Satan is wandering like a ferocious lion who wants to eat. The devil does not joke, but can deceive us with gentleness and tricks because it is his nature to use deceit, as we know he did with Eve. Yet, on the cross, Christ publicly exposed the devil's wickedness and triumphed over him. By forgiving the thief on His right hand and welcoming him into Paradise, Christ demonstrated His power to overcome sin and death.

Through the imagery of the Passover lamb, believers are reminded of the protective power of Christ's blood and are encouraged to mark their hearts with the cross. We look at Christ and say to Him: "Yesterday we were overwhelmed by your humility and the life that You gave us, but today we are seeing You saving us with Your blood." At the end of the praise we have been using this week, we say: "The Lord is my strength, and my praise, He has become my sacred salvation. My Lord, Jesus Christ, my good saviour."

Today is a day of victory, not just mourning and sadness. While there may be mourning in some homes due to the loss of loved ones, we do not mourn here for we are promised that our sorrow will be transformed to joy. Though sadness exists in the world, we possess joy that non-believers do not comprehend. In a similar way, the people of Israel experienced happiness tonight. Imagine if one of them had not marked their house's poles with blood. What would have befallen them? The angel of death would have struck that house and claimed their firstborn. That is the peril faced by a soul in today's world which is not shielded by the blood of Christ; such a soul is treated no differently than one oblivious to Christ's salvation. The angel of death passes over souls marked with the blood, which is why we strive to be immersed in Christ's blood. Isaiah the prophet writes: "Why is Your apparel red,

And Your garments like one who treads in the winepress? 'I have trodden the winepress alone, And from the peoples no one was with Me'" (Isaiah 63:2-3). Without this blood, we are valueless.

The Passover wasn't merely a one-time event based on escaping Pharoah, but an ongoing experience for the Israelites. When confronted by giants skilled in warfare, Moses, troubled, sought the Lord's guidance. The Lord instructed Moses to keep his arms raised, reminiscent of the cross, and pray continuously to ensure victory. When the Israelites were bitten by snakes, Moses was instructed to raise a copper snake on a rod, resembling a cross. Whenever they forgot, they faltered. Similarly, the Pascha remains relevant in our lives today, "For indeed Christ, our Passover, was sacrificed for us" (1 Corinthians 5:7). Therefore, let us celebrate the Pascha not only annually after the Lent season but embrace its significance in our daily existence. Satan persists, and so does our human weakness; the blood stands before us daily, supporting every battle against sin as long as our lives are marked by the blood.

If our ancestors endured slavery under Pharaoh, Satan, and his cohorts, while we relish freedom now, we must taste a bit of bitterness to empathise with their plight. This inevitably comes in the form of bitterness of struggling

Good Friday

in sin, bitterness of laziness, or bitterness of lacking... so how should we endure? If Christ is our Passover, then let us partake of it with readiness, urgency, and resolve. We witness this by seeing the monks' practice of girding themselves for prayer, adopting a straight posture of active engagement. Christ admonished us this week to strive and enter through the narrow door. These teachings, though bitter, are essential components of our daily Pascha.

The work of God demands strength, not feeble hands. "Cursed is he who does the work of the Lord deceitfully" (Jeremiah 48:10). Scripture warns against laziness or deceit in carrying out God's work. Prayer should be fervent, not careless; our posture should be steadfast as we partake of Christ. Laziness is insidious; it starts subtly but escalates. Neglecting prayer may lead to apathy toward church attendance, confession, and scripture reading. Eventually, lukewarmness becomes our normal way of life. On judgment day, God will not only condemn sinners but also the lazy. Complaining about bitterness only detracts from its transformative power. God's work is swift. Therefore, eat with urgency, with shoes on, rod in hand, and with a heart committed to spiritual activity.

Let us be glad knowing that the angel of death passes over us. There will come a final Pascha when we depart from this earth, a crossing where those not protected by Christ's blood dread death, haunted by the shadows of demons eager to drag them to hell. But the believers, those who have embraced Christ, look forward to being welcomed by angels and St Mary herself. Therefore, let us dwell before the cross, drawing spiritual sustenance from the blood that flowed from it, just like Mary Magdalene illustrated beneath the cross. Unlike the disciples who fled at the sight of Christ's blood, let us spiritually partake in His sacrifice. and recognize that our communion with Christ transcends our time on this earth.

Christ is our Pascha, our sacrificial lamb. This week, He liberated captives in hell, he offered hope to the despairing, and cleanses every sin with his blood, ensuring our safe journey through life's bitterness and temptations. Let us celebrate His resurrection throughout our lives, and into eternity.

To the Lord is the power and glory forever and ever, Amen.

www.ingramcontent.com/pod-product-compliance
Lightning Source LLC
Chambersburg PA
CBHW032136090426
42743CB00007B/611